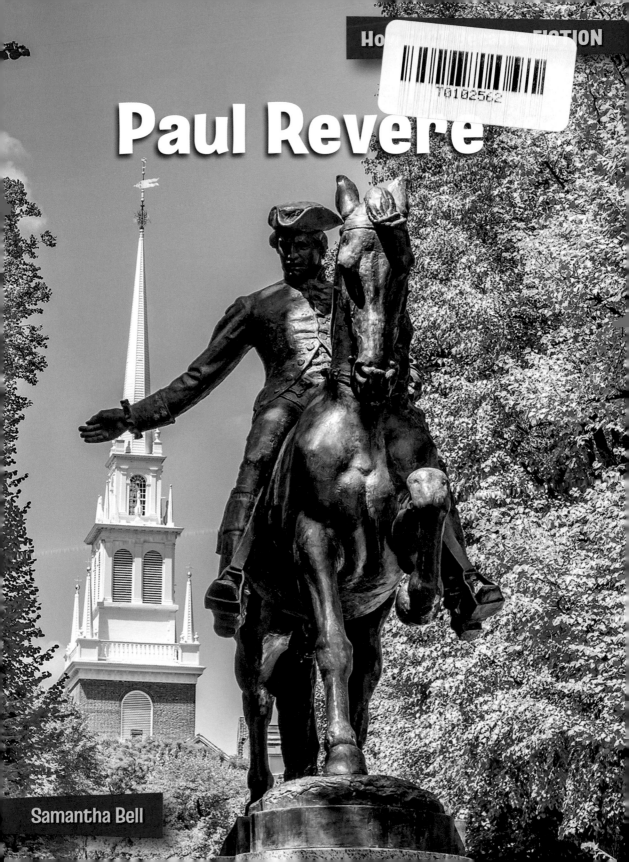

Paul Revere

Samantha Bell

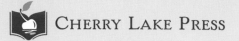
CHERRY LAKE PRESS

Published in the United States of America by Cherry Lake Publishing Group
Ann Arbor, Michigan
www.cherrylakepublishing.com

Reading Adviser: Beth Walker Gambro, MS, Ed., Reading Consultant, Yorkville, IL

Photo Credits: © f11photo/Shutterstock, cover, title page; John Singleton Copley, Public domain, via Wikimedia Commons, 5; Grant Wood, Public domain, via Wikimedia Commons, 6; © HDnrg/Shutterstock, 7; © Benjamin Clapp/Shutterstock, 8; Hy Hintermeister (This could be by either John Henry Hintermeister (1869-1945) or his son Henry Hintermeister (1897-1970). Neither the copyright register nor the signature gives a clue which painter made the work.), Public domain, via Wikimedia Commons, 9; The National Guard, Public domain, via Wikimedia Commons, 10; Edward Mason Eggleston (1882-1941), Public domain, via Wikimedia Commons, 11; British Cartoon Prints Collection, Library of Congress, Prints and Photographs Division, 13; Sons of Liberty, Public domain, via Wikimedia Commons, 14; Matthewconti, CC BY-SA 4.0 via Wikimedia Commons, 15; The original uploader was Pitchka at English Wikipedia., Public domain, via Wikimedia Commons, 17; Office of War Information, Public domain, via Wikimedia Commons, 18; Architect of the Capitol, Public domain, via Wikimedia Commons, 19; Popular Graphic Arts, Library of Congress, Prints and Photographs Division, 21; National Portrait Gallery, Smithsonian Institution; gift of Thomas P. Curtis and Elizabeth Longfellow Kohler in memory of Elizabeth Longfellow Curtis, 22; Tichnor Bros. Inc., Boston, Mass., Public domain, via Wikimedia Commons, 23; © Jorge Salcedo/Shutterstock, 24; © Jorge Salcedo/Shutterstock, 25; © Conny Pokorny/Shutterstock, 27; National Archives and Records Administration, Public domain, via Wikimedia Commons, 28; William Barnes Wollen, Public domain, via Wikimedia Commons, 30

Cherry Lake Press is an imprint of Cherry Lake Publishing Group.

Library of Congress Cataloging-in-Publication Data has been filed and is available at catalog.loc.gov.

Cherry Lake Publishing Group would like to acknowledge the work of the Partnership for 21st Century Learning, a Network of Battelle for Kids. Please visit http://www.battelleforkids.org/networks/p21 for more information.

Printed in the United States of America
Corporate Graphics

Note from publisher: Websites change regularly, and their future contents are outside of our control. Supervise children when conducting any recommended online searches for extended learning opportunities.

Samantha Bell was born and raised near Orlando, Florida. She grew up in a family of eight kids and all kinds of pets, including goats, chickens, cats, dogs, rabbits, horses, parakeets, hamsters, guinea pigs, a monkey, a raccoon, and a coatimundi. She now lives with her family in the foothills of the Blue Ridge Mountains, where she enjoys hiking, painting, and snuggling with their cats Pocket, Pebble, and Mr. Tree-Tree Triggers.

CONTENTS

CHAPTER 1

The Story People Tell

The British Are Coming

In the years leading up to the American Revolution (1775–1783), Paul Revere worked as a **silversmith**. He had his own shop in Boston, Massachusetts. At the time, tensions were high between the colonists and the British soldiers. Many of the colonists were growing tired of the British laws and taxes. They had no **representation** in the British government that ruled them. Known as Patriots, these colonists wanted to be free from Britain. Revere was a Patriot, and he was ready to help.

Paul Revere worked as a silversmith in the years leading up to the American Revolution.

In 1774 and 1775, Revere became an express rider for the Patriots. He carried news, messages, and important documents on horseback. On the evening of April 18, 1775, a Patriot named Dr. Joseph Warren called on Revere. Warren told Revere that the British troops would soon be on the move. They planned to arrest two Patriot leaders, Samuel Adams and John Hancock. The men were meeting in Lexington, Massachusetts. Revere was to ride to Lexington and warn them. Then he was to ride on to the town of Concord. The Patriots had stored weapons and **gunpowder** there. If the British got there first, they would take it all.

The tower of the Old North Church in Boston

Revere contacted a friend to help. The friend would watch the British Army to see which direction they would go. Then he was to go up into the tower of the Old North Church in Boston. He would signal Revere with a lantern. If the British were going by land, he would hold up one lantern. If they were crossing the river, he would hold up two lanterns. That way, Revere would know which route he should take.

The story says Revere's friend saw the British Army start marching toward the water. He signaled for Revere to ride!

Revere's friend watched and waited. Then he saw the British Army begin to march toward the water. They were crossing the river. The friend held up two lights. That was the signal for Revere to ride. He raced out of Boston on his horse. First, he rode to Lexington to warn Adams and Hancock. The story says that along the way,

People say that Revere sped on his horse from Boston to Lexington to warn Samuel Adams and John Hancock of the British troops.

THE SHOT HEARD AROUND THE WORLD

In Lexington, Paul Revere alerted Captain John Parker that the British were on their way. Parker was the commander of the Lexington **militia**. Around sunrise, the British marched into town. The militia were waiting on Lexington Green. This was open, shared land in the center of town. The colonists were outnumbered by the British 80 to 400. Parker was not planning on fighting. But the British left the road and met the colonists on the Green. They ordered the Patriots to **disperse**. Captain Parker gave the same order. He knew they could not win. But in the confusion, someone fired a **musket**. Then both sides began shooting. The revolution had begun. That first shot fired came to be known as "the shot heard 'round the world."

People say Revere woke people with the alarm "The British are coming! The British are coming!"

he yelled out, "The British are coming! The British are coming!" People woke up to the alarm. Some of them were Minutemen. These volunteer soldiers were well-trained. They were ready to fight on a minute's notice. Revere rode on to Concord. He did not stop until everyone had been warned and the weapons were safe.

CHAPTER 2

The Facts of the Matter

The Regulars Are Coming

Many students have heard the story of Paul Revere riding through the night to warn the colonists. It can be found in almost every U.S. history book. But people often remember the legendary story instead of the actual events. Revere did not just warn the colonists and get them out of bed. His ride was part of an elaborate alarm system. It kept the British from taking the colonists' **stockpile** of weapons.

Paul Revere was a member of the Sons of Liberty. This was a secret society of Patriots. They formed in 1765 with two chapters. One was in New York, and the other was in Boston. By 1775, there were chapters in all 13 of the colonies. The Sons of Liberty not only opposed British rule. They also often used fear and even violence to resist it. Revere had a printing

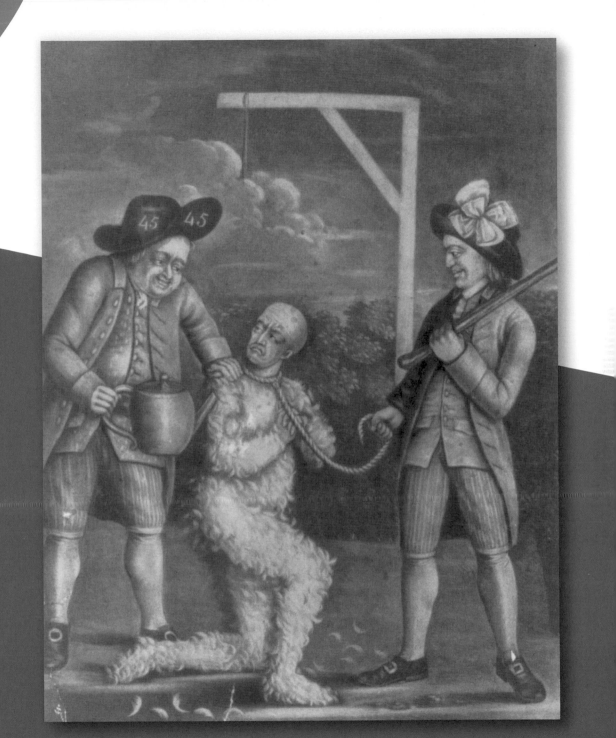

It was known that the Sons of Liberty tarred and feathered British officials. They often used fear and violence to resist British rule.

St—p! St—p! St—p! No:

Tuesday-Morning, December 17, 1765.

THE True-born Sons of Liberty, are desired to meet under LIBERTY-TREE, at XII o'Clock, THIS DAY, to hear the the public Resignation, under Oath, of ANDREW OLIVER, Esq; Distributor of Stamps for the Province of the Massachusetts-Bay.

A publication from the Sons of Liberty identifies a meeting place under the Liberty Tree, a famous elm tree in Boston. Loyalists cut the tree down in 1775.

press in his silversmith shop. He used it to print materials for the Sons of Liberty. They wanted to influence the colonists against the British. Revere also served as a messenger. British soldiers had been stationed in Boston since 1768. Revere would travel from Boston to other colonies on horseback. He provided the leaders with news from Boston. He also brought them information about the British Army.

In April 1775, General Thomas Gage commanded the British troops in Boston. He learned that the Patriots were storing gunpowder and weapons in Concord. Concord was about 20 miles (32 kilometers) away. Gage decided to send about 700 soldiers on a secret mission.

They were to march to Concord in the middle of the night and take the weapons. The British hoped it would put an end to any plans of rebellion.

With Samuel Adams away in Lexington, Dr. Joseph Warren became the Patriot leader in Boston. Patriot spies had informed him the British would be marching soon. Warren thought they were going to Lexington to arrest Hancock and Adams. He suspected they might take the weapons at Concord, too.

ONE IF BY LAND, TWO IF BY SEA

Revere and other Patriots met the Sunday before the march on Concord. They planned the signal they would use. They decided on lanterns in the steeple of the Old North Church. If the British were going out by land, there would be one lantern. If they went out by water, there would be two. That way, all of the messengers would know the direction the British were moving. Before he rode off, Revere confirmed that they had seen the signals.

General Gage decided to move his troops the night of April 18. Warren heard of his plan. Warren sent for Paul Revere and a man named William Dawes. Revere was to row across the Charles River. Then he would ride on to Lexington. Dawes was to take a longer route. He would meet up with Revere in Lexington. They would warn Hancock and Adams. Then they would ride on to Concord together. Other messengers would be riding as well. Among these was Israel Bissell, who rode 345 miles (555 km) over 4 days from Massachusetts to Philadelphia warning the militias that war had started.

William Dawes's route was more difficult. It had British checkpoints. Dawes was chosen for this route because he did not cause trouble. He was a leather tanner. He often had to leave town past checkpoints. The guards would recognize him. They wouldn't be suspicious.

Revere had already arranged the lantern signals with his friend. He crossed the river, passing by a British warship. He arrived safely on the other side. Then he mounted his horse and started toward Lexington. Dawes had already gone another way. As the two men rode through the towns, they handed off their message to more riders. Riders spread the word as far away as Connecticut and New Hampshire.

William Dawes's route to Lexington was far more difficult than Paul Revere's.

Some depictions of Revere have him riding with a whip, pushing his horse as fast as it could go.

Around midnight, Revere arrived in Lexington. He went to warn Hancock and Adams. A Patriot guard told him to be quiet in case they were asleep. But Revere shouted, "You'll have noise enough before long. The regulars are coming out!" Dawes arrived about 30 minutes later. Revere and Dawes then continued to Concord. At the same time, Dr. Samuel Prescott was heading home from Lexington to Concord. He was part of the Sons of Liberty. He caught up with Revere and Dawes. He helped them warn families along the way.

A short time later, two British officers on horseback surprised the three men. Revere was riding in front. He was captured, but Dawes and Prescott escaped. Revere was questioned and later let go. He returned to Lexington in time to see part of the battle.

CHAPTER 3

Spinning the Story

The Midnight Ride

The ride to warn Lexington and Concord was as important as it was dangerous. Not only did the men alert Hancock and Adams, but they also succeeded in warning the people of Concord. Most of the weapons and gunpowder had been moved by the time the British arrived. After it was over, Revere's story grew even bigger. Newspapers and pamphlets told about the mission. Within 3 weeks, articles about Revere's ride were in newspapers in New York, Philadelphia, and Baltimore. Many other riders were involved in the mission. But Revere was the only one mentioned. People already knew he was an express rider. His reputation as a Patriot continued to grow.

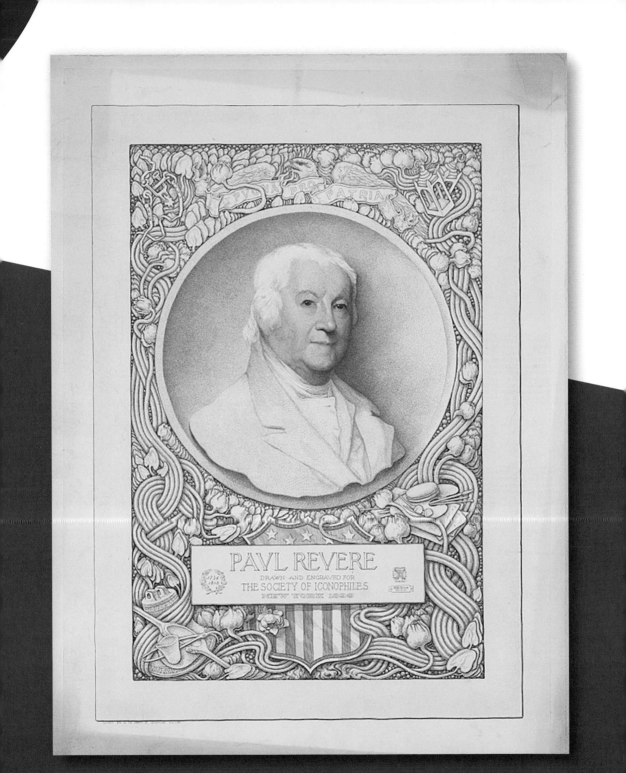

Paul Revere's reputation as a Patriot only grew after his midnight ride.

Henry Wadsworth Longfellow was a famous poet in his own time. He was one of the most well-known American poets of the 19th century.

Paul Revere's Ride

(IN PART)
HENRY WADSWORTH LONGFELLOW

Listen, my children, and you shall hear
Of the midnight ride of Paul Revere,
On the eighteenth of April, in Seventy-five;
Hardly a man is now alive
Who remembers that famous day and year.

He said to his friend, "If the British march
By land or sea from the town to-night,
Hang a lantern aloft in the belfry arch
Of the North Church tower as a signal light,-
One if by land, and two if by sea;
And I on the opposite shore will be,
Ready to ride and spread the alarm
Through every Middlesex village and farm,
For the country folk to be up and to arm."

You know the rest. In the books you have read
How the British Regulars fired and fled,—
How the farmers gave them ball for ball,
From behind each fence and farmyard wall,
Chasing the redcoats down the lane,
Then crossing the fields to emerge again
Under the trees at the turn of the road,
And only pausing to fire and load.

So through the night rode Paul Revere;
And so through the night went his cry of alarm
To every Middlesex village and farm,—
A cry of defiance, and not of fear,
A voice in the darkness, a knock at the door,
And a word that shall echo for evermore !

Paul Revere House

"Paul Revere's Ride" became a famous poem.

In 1860, poet Henry Wadsworth Longfellow wrote about Revere's heroic act. His poem is called "Paul Revere's Ride." It was published in *The Atlantic Monthly* magazine in January 1861. In the poem, Revere rides alone to warn the colonists. Some parts of the poem are exaggerated. It also leaves out some historical facts. But Longfellow was not trying to give a historical account. The poem was meant to create a true American hero.

Longfellow was strongly against slavery. He viewed it as opposing the American principles of freedom and justice. Slavery had become one of the most divisive issues in the nation. The Northern and Southern states would soon be caught up in the Civil War (1861–1865). Longfellow wrote his poem during this time of crisis. He hoped his poem would

TRY, TRY AGAIN

Paul Revere's ride has been **commemorated** in other ways. Statues of Revere have been erected in his honor. One of the most famous is in Boston, Massachusetts. A competition for the statue started in 1883. A 22-year-old sculptor named Cyrus Dallin was selected. But he had to submit five to seven versions of his idea. It was not until 1899 before the judges agreed on a design. The bronze statue was finally finished in 1940. It was placed in front of the Old North Church. It shows Paul Revere on horseback as he rides through the streets.

The tower of Old North Church (where the signal lanterns hung)
can be seen behind the Boston statue of Paul Revere.

inspire a feeling of **patriotism** and unity among the American people. He wanted the story of Paul Revere to remind them of the country's noble past. It became one of Longfellow's most well-known poems. In the years after its publication, people began to think of it as historical fact.

CHAPTER 4

Writing History

Comparing Accounts

Historians have a lot of resources for discovering the true story of Paul Revere's ride. Many documents from that time are available. They provide a lot of information. Even though the newspaper articles only mention Revere, they are still good sources. Other documents include letters, diaries, and journals. Some documents were even written by Revere himself.

For example, in 1775, Revere wrote a report to the Massachusetts Provincial Congress. The Congress wanted **testimonials** from colonists about the events at Lexington. They wanted to know who fired first. If witnesses agreed that the British had fired first, then the Patriots' actions would be seen as self-defense. That way, they could get more support from colonists who were still unsure of what side to support. Revere sent in one copy of his testimonial.

The Minute Man statue was finished in 1874 by sculptor Daniel Chester French. It stands in Minute Man National Historical Park (Concord) today at one end of North Bridge, where the "shot heard 'round the world" was fired.

Though many believe it was a one-man show, Paul Revere's famous ride happened with a coordinated communication effort of many colonists.

Then he decided to change some things and sent it in again. Both testimonials are available for historians to study. The differences between them are very small. The second one also includes some spelling and grammatical corrections.

Around 1798, a man named Jeremy Belknap wrote to Paul Revere. Belknap was a historian with the Massachusetts Historical Society. He asked Revere to tell about his activities on April 18 again. Revere's letter retold the story of his famous ride. He mentioned Dr. Joseph Warren. He told how Warren encouraged

Revere to ride to Lexington. He talked about how he made plans with other Patriots to use lanterns as signals. Other details included how two friends rowed him across the Charles River as the moon was starting to rise. He mentioned a narrow escape from a couple of British soldiers before he reached Lexington. Revere's letter to Belknap was written 23 years after the famous ride. But the facts are the same as his earlier reports.

Paul Revere's ride was more than just one man carrying a warning. It was an example of the well-coordinated efforts of the colonists. Because of their communication and planning, the Patriots were ready for the British that night.

IT'S ALL IN THE DETAILS

Some details of an event can only be told by the people who were there. For example, in his letter to Belknap, Revere talks about meeting Dr. Prescott near Lexington. Revere mentioned to Prescott that they should warn all the people on the way to Concord. Prescott thought it was a good idea. He decided to go with Revere and Dawes, since he lived in Concord. The people there knew him. If he was with Revere and Dawes, the people there would believe what they were saying. These types of details make firsthand reports so valuable to historians.

Activity

What Happened Next?

When the British reached Concord, most of the firearms and gunpowder was gone. But that's not the end of the story. What did the British do next? With the help of a teacher, parent, or librarian, do some research about the Battle of Lexington and Concord. Then write a short report on what you learn.

Learn More

Books

Doeden, Matt. *The Colonists Revolt.* North Mankato, MN: Capstone Press, 2019.

Haugen, Brenda. *The Split History of the Battles of Lexington and Concord: A Perspectives Flip Book.* North Mankato, MN: Compass Point Books, 2018.

Min, Ellen. *The Midnight Ride of Paul Revere: One if by Land, Two if by Sea.* New York, NY: PowerKids Press, 2016.

Troupe, Thomas Kingsley. *Paul Revere's Ride.* North Mankato, MN: Picture Window Books, 2017.

On the Web

With an adult, explore more online with these suggested searches.

"1770: The American Revolution," Mission US: For Crown or Colony? Online Game

"Paul Revere's Ride," American Battlefield Trust

"The Midnight Rides of April 18 & 19, 1775: Interactive Map," The Paul Revere House

"The Real Story of Paul Revere's Ride," The Paul Revere House

Glossary

commemorated (kuh-MEH-muh-ray-tuhd) served as a reminder or memorial

disperse (dih-SPUHRS) to drive away or scatter in all directions

gunpowder (GUHN-pow-duhr) an explosive used to propel a bullet from a gun

militia (muh-LIH-shuh) a group of military-trained civilians, usually used only in emergencies

musket (MUH-skuht) a large, heavy gun with a large barrel that was loaded through the muzzle

patriotism (PAY-tree-uh-tih-zuhm) love for and devotion to one's country

representation (reh-prih-zen-TAY-shuhn) an arrangement whereby an individual can speak or act on behalf of someone else

silversmith (SIL-vuhr-smith) someone who creates or repairs items made of silver

stockpile (STAHK-py-uhl) a supply of items gathered for future use

testimonials (teh-stuh-MOH-nee-uhls) accounts of events

Index